HOT TOPICS

IMMIGRATION

Nick Hunter

Chicago, Illinois

www.heinemannraintree.com
Visit our website to find out
more information about
Heinemann-Raintree books.

To order:
☎ Phone 888-454-2279
▭ Visit www.heinemannraintree.com
to browse our catalog and order online.

© 2012 Heinemann Library
an imprint of Capstone Global Library, LLC
Chicago, Illinois

Visit our website at www.heinemannraintree.
com

Edited by Adam Miller, Andrew Farrow, and
Jennifer Locke
Designed by Clare Webber and Steven Mead
Original illustrations © Capstone Global Library
Ltd.
Picture research by Ruth Blair
Production by Eirian Griffiths
Originated by Capstone Global Library Ltd.
Printed and bound in China by Leo Paper
Group Ltd.

16 15 14 13 12
10 9 8 7 6 5 4 3 2 1

**Library of Congress
Cataloging-in-Publication Data**
Hunter, Nick.
  Immigration / Nick Hunter.
    p. cm.—(Hot topics)
  Includes bibliographical references
and index.
  ISBN 978-1-4329-5175-7 (hc)
  1. Emigration and immigration.
  2. Immigrants. 3. Illegal aliens. I. Title.
  JV6201.H88 2012
  304.8—dc22   2010044765

Acknowledgments
The author and publishers are grateful to
the following for permission to reproduce
copyright material: Alamy pp. **5** (© Norma Jean
Gargasz), **14** (© vario images GmbH & Co.
KG), **21** (© swedish images), **31** (© Warren
Diggles), **33** (© Jeffrey Blackler); Corbis pp.
6 (© Bettmann), **9** (© Janet Jarman), **11**, **12**
(© Stephen Morrison/epa), **13** (© BRAUCHLI
DAVID), **16** (© Gideon Mendel), **18** (© CAREN
FIROUZ/Reuters), **27** (© Catherine Karnow),
28 (© Peter Ginter/Science Faction), **35** (©
Manjunath Kiran/epa), **37** (© Christopher
Morris), **47** (© DARRIN ZAMMIT LUPI/Reuters),
45 (© EPA/LARRY W. SMITH); Getty Images
pp. **4** (Alberto Rosado), **38** (AFP), **40** (Alex
Wong), **41** (Keystone), **42** (DENIS CHARLET/
AFP); Shutterstock pp. **10** (© leungchopan), **22**
(© sepavo), **49** (© Philip Lange).

Cover photograph of a Mexican man holding
onto the fence that separates the U.S.-Mexico
border reproduced with the permission of
Corbis (© Carlos Cazalis).

We would like to thank Kristen Kowalkowski
for her invaluable help in the preparation of
this book.

Every effort has been made to contact
copyright holders of any material reproduced
in this book. Any omissions will be rectified in
subsequent printings if notice is given to the
publisher.

CONTENTS

Some words are printed in bold, **like this**. You can find out what they mean by looking in the glossary.

CROSSING THE BORDER

The Guerrero family stopped to rest before the final leg of their journey. They made a makeshift shelter out of plastic sheeting left by others who had passed this way before. Mario, his pregnant wife, Oralia, and their young son knew there were many dangers lying ahead on the eight-hour walk to the U.S. border. They would have to watch out for the U.S. border guards, planes, and helicopters that were on the lookout for Mexican **migrants**. They would have to avoid the warring drug-smuggling gangs of the area, and deal with the heat of the desert and natural dangers like scorpions and snakes. They were sure it would all be worth it when they reached the United States.

■ Migrants take huge risks crossing the Straits of Gibraltar from Morocco to Spain.

Dangerous journeys

Across the world, many people set out on journeys just as dangerous as the Guerreros' trek from Mexico to the United States. In southern Europe, hopeful migrants from Africa try to cross the 8 miles (12 kilometers) of the dangerous Straits of Gibraltar in tiny boats. Many do not complete their journey. Some are picked up by Spanish patrols or rescued when their boats capsize in the strong currents. Others are not so lucky, and their bodies are washed up on the shore days later.

■ Thousands of Mexican immigrants cross the desert every year in search of a new life.

Many of these people put themselves in the hands of smugglers who will organize their journey to a new home. Some journeys are long and complicated, like the Chinese workers who travel across land in the backs of trucks to jobs in London and other European cities, or aboard container ships from Hong Kong to Los Angeles.

A better life?

The people who take these journeys are called migrants. They are moving to live and work in another country. Many migrants are within the law: They have been given the right to move to a new country. Others, like the examples above, are illegal migrants. They have to take huge risks to get across the border into their new country.

Why do people risk their lives and those of their families to move to a new country? These people must have powerful reasons for wanting to move. This book will look at why people **migrate** and their experiences when they arrive in a new country. We will also consider the effects of migration on the countries themselves. Which countries do people move to, and do migrants benefit those countries? What happens to the countries they leave behind? Is there too much immigration into your country? Why is it such a hot topic?

WHAT IS IMMIGRATION?

Any movement of people to live in a new home is called migration. Immigration refers to the movement of people into a particular country, such as immigration into the United States from Mexico. When people leave their home country, this is called emigration.

WHY DO PEOPLE MIGRATE?

Migration has been happening throughout history. It is likely that your **ancestors** were **immigrants** into your home country at one time or another. The nations of Europe were formed by people who invaded and settled in those countries hundreds or even thousands of years ago. Settlers to the United Kingdom included Romans, Anglo-Saxons, Vikings, and Normans. Many of the people of North America are descended from people who migrated from Europe or were transported from Africa as slaves. European settlers also migrated to countries like Australia and South Africa. Only **indigenous** people who first settled lands such as North America and Australia can really claim not to be descended from immigrants.

European settlers who migrated to North America were often trying to escape extreme **poverty** or **persecution** for their religious beliefs or **culture**. The "New World" offered the prospect of escaping from the prejudices and hardships of their homelands. For many people, migration held the promise of a new life and new opportunities.

■ Many European immigrants settled in neighborhoods like New York's Lower East Side.

6

"Why should Pennsylvania, founded by the English, become a Colony of Aliens [foreigners], who will shortly be so numerous as to Germanize us instead of our Anglifying them, and will never adopt our Language or Customs ...?"

American statesman Benjamin Franklin complains about German immigration to Pennsylvania in 1751

Modern migration

Since 1945 many people have migrated from poorer and **developing countries** to **developed countries** in Europe, North America, and elsewhere. In the past, migration often meant a long sea journey and leaving their homeland behind forever. Although some migrants still take long and difficult journeys, international air travel and instant communication by phone and Internet make it much easier for people to keep in touch with their homeland.

The reasons why migrants have moved are not too different from the reasons why people moved in the past. People move to work or to earn more money than they can in their own countries. They feel that migration will create a better future for their children. Some people migrate because they are fleeing war and persecution.

The immigration debate

As long as people have been moving around, there have been debates about immigration. Many people feel that there should be stricter limits on immigration because immigrants may change the culture of the country they move to or take jobs that would otherwise go to those who were born there. Others think that immigrants bring many benefits to a country. Attitudes and restrictions are a major factor in people's decisions about where to migrate.

Economic migrants

Most people migrate to another country because they believe they will be able to earn more money in their new home or at least escape from extreme poverty. These people are called economic migrants. Some of these economic migrants choose to settle permanently in another country. Others move for a few years to earn enough money to start a business or buy a house in their home country. Some people migrate every year to earn money in seasonal work such as picking fruit or helping with the harvest.

Earning power

The main reason why there are so many economic migrants is because there are big differences in what people can earn for doing the same kind of work in different parts of the world. A U.S. factory worker earns around four times as much as someone doing the same job in Mexico. Mexican farmworkers also earn much less than those in the United States. The two countries share a border of nearly 2,000 miles (3,140 kilometers), so it is no surprise that many Mexicans try to enter the United States. Some are able to get permission to work legally. Many more take the dangerous journey to cross the border illegally.

There are many other parts of the world with similar differences in earnings between countries. Citizens of the European Union (EU) are able to move freely to live and work in any country of the EU. Many workers from eastern EU countries, such as Poland, can earn more in other European countries like Germany and the United Kingdom. This has led to a lot of migration within the EU. It also means that someone from outside the EU who gains entry into one European country can move freely across Europe.

Although the differences in earnings between countries may tempt workers to migrate, people also have to consider whether work will be available in their new country. Jobs are likely to be easier to find when the economy of a country is doing well. When the economy is doing badly, fewer jobs are available and people may earn less money than in the past. Many countries, including the United States and the United Kingdom, suffered difficult economic conditions in the years after 2008. Many eastern European workers who had moved to the United Kingdom to work chose to return home because they could no longer find work so easily.

There is still a big demand for migrant workers to pick fruit. Many areas of farming are now done by machines, but fruits are often too soft to pick by machines.

WHY DON'T MORE PEOPLE MIGRATE?

It is easy to understand why people would move to a country where they could earn much more money than in their home country. It may even seem surprising that more people don't migrate to other countries. There are many other factors that people have to consider when they choose to move:

- Family ties: Migration may mean leaving behind family and friends, or it may involve uprooting the family and taking them to a new country.
- Cultural ties: Moving to a new country may mean adapting to a very different culture and way of life.
- Dangers: Although many people migrate legally, there are others who choose to take difficult and dangerous journeys to reach their chosen country.
- Benefits: Work may pay better, but contracts may be short, and illegal immigrants will not get the same benefits and protections as other workers.

Three Ds

Much of the work that is done by economic migrants is often called the "three Ds" because the jobs are difficult, dirty, and dangerous. These jobs are usually not well paid and are less attractive to other workers. However, immigrants from poorer countries can sometimes earn more by doing these jobs than they could working jobs that require more skills in their home countries. Construction is one of the main areas where immigrants are employed. Other areas include farming and personal services such as cleaning and gardening.

Skilled migrants

Not all immigrants move to do "three Ds" work. Many economic migrants are well educated and skilled in areas like health care and information technology (IT). They move because their skills might be in more demand or better paid in other countries. Many countries will try hard to attract immigrants to do particular jobs. This is usually because they do not have enough skilled people in their native population to do the jobs. According to the U.S. Census Bureau, in 2008, 27 percent of all physicians in the United States were immigrants. Other countries are no different—25 percent of nurses in London were born overseas.

■ Major centers of business like Hong Kong attract skilled economic migrants to work in banks and corporations. They also attract migrants to work in poorly paid jobs in hotels and restaurants that service these people.

Many of the world's largest corporations have offices in different countries. Sometimes their employees will take jobs in different countries. Some of these people will settle and become citizens of their new countries; others will return to their country of birth after a few years or move on to somewhere new.

Some economic migrants leave families behind, sending home some of their earnings to support their families. Other economic migrants move with wives or husbands and children. These immigrants, who depend on the person who is moving to work, are not necessarily looking for work but want services like schools and health care.

■ One of the most extreme examples of highly **skilled migrants** are sports stars whose skills enable them to get paid millions and move far away from their countries of birth. Soccer star Didier Drogba plays for Chelsea Football Club in London but was born on the Ivory Coast in West Africa.

Money is the goal for economic migrants. Other migrants are motivated by different reasons. For example, retired people from northern European countries, like the United Kingdom and Germany, may choose to move to Spain and Portugal because they are warmer. This type of migration also happens in the United States, but retired migrants do not have to leave their own country to find warmer weather in Florida, Arizona, and California.

Environmental migration

In the next few decades, we are likely to see a new type of economic migrant. Most scientists agree that Earth's climate is changing due to humans' impact on the environment. If climate change continues, sea levels are likely to rise and flood coastal areas where many people live. Desert regions where food cannot be grown will spread. These changes will mean that more people will not have access to enough food and water. This will put pressures on many of the world's poorest countries. It will force more people to try and move to countries where they can earn enough money to live. Rising sea levels and spreading deserts will also put pressure on resources in richer countries.

Refugees and asylum seekers

Every year many of the people who migrate to another country are forced to leave their homes because they fear for their lives. **Refugees** have to flee from war or from persecution because of race, religion, political views, or belonging to a particular social group.

They often have to leave with just what they can carry. Refugee crises because of wars and natural disasters can mean that whole populations have to move very quickly.

Some refugees will stay in their new country, but many will return to their home countries when they are able to—although this can take years if they are fleeing from a political regime that is persecuting them.

■ Children, like these refugees fleeing the conflict in the Darfur region of Sudan, also have to bear the hardships of war.

When does an economic migrant become a refugee?

The **United Nations** Convention on Refugees was signed in 1951. It guarantees refugees' rights not to be returned to the country they came from, as their lives may be in danger. In recent years, many countries have started to use the term *asylum seeker* to describe people who are claiming to be refugees. Immigration authorities believed that many who said they were refugees were actually economic migrants. Claiming refugee status was the only way they could move legally to their new country. Asylum seekers are only classified as refugees once they are given the right to live in the new country.

Refugees from Kosovo were forced to flee to other European countries because of conflict in 1999.

REFUGEE CRISES

Most of the biggest refugee crises have been caused by war and internal conflicts. In the twenty-first century, refugees have mainly come from Afghanistan, Iraq, and African countries including Somalia, Sudan, and the Democratic Republic of Congo. Although refugees from these crises may go to a number of countries, most travel to the nearest place of safety. The countries that are home to most refugees are Pakistan and Iran. It is also possible to be a refugee in your own country. Fighting and devastating floods in northwest Pakistan forced hundreds of thousands of Pakistanis and Afghan refugees to leave the area in 2009 and 2010.

CASE STUDY

Refugee crisis: Afghanistan

Afghanistan has been the scene of a series of bloody conflicts since it was invaded by the Soviet Union in 1979. Afghan fighters defeated the invaders, but this war was followed by a bitter struggle between different **factions** to control the country. The brutal **Taliban** came to power in 1996. The Taliban follow an extreme form of Islam that prevents women from going to school and imposes harsh punishments for anyone who does not live by their strict laws.

These decades of conflict led millions of people to become refugees in neighboring countries. In late 2001, the United States, United Kingdom, and their allies invaded Afghanistan to overthrow the Taliban government. In the years that followed, around 5 million refugees returned to Afghanistan, despite the ongoing conflict between US-led forces and the Taliban.

Although millions of refugees had returned, there were still more refugees from Afghanistan than any other country in 2009. Almost 3 million Afghans lived in 73 different countries. Most were in neighboring Pakistan and Iran.

■ The destruction of war always results in people losing their homes as this housing complex in Kabul, Afghanistan, shows.

A refugee's story

Teenager Hashmat Suddat left Kabul, the Afghan capital, with his sisters and younger brother in 2000. They fled to Pakistan, fearful of the Taliban government and the continuing war that had led to the deaths of Hashmat's parents. After nine months in a camp on the Pakistan border, the family was given refugee status. "It's a really bad experience to leave your homeland. Where you were born, lived ... your community," said Hashmat. "We were happy to get out of there, but everybody cried when we got the letter that stated we were accepted as refugees." In late 2001, the family arrived in the United States. Hashmat was able to graduate from high school in Richmond, Virginia, in 2003 and went on to college to study computer science. One day, Hashmat hopes to be able to return to his homeland to help educate others.

Resettling refugees

The United Nations High Commissioner for Refugees (UNHCR) works with a number of other charities, such as the Red Cross, to meet the needs of refugees. This includes helping refugees return to Afghanistan to find work, shelter, and enough food. The flow of refugees back to their homes is slowing because of the continuing conflict, and because many refugees have been absent for so long, they have very little to return to.

Since 2009, conflict in the border areas between Pakistan and Afghanistan has caused about 2 million Pakistanis to seek refuge elsewhere in the country.

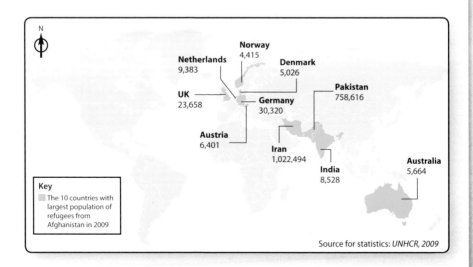

N

Norway
4,415

Netherlands
9,383

Denmark
5,026

Pakistan
758,616

UK
23,658

Germany
30,320

Austria
6,401

Iran
1,022,494

India
8,528

Australia
5,664

Key
The 10 countries with largest population of refugees from Afghanistan in 2009

Source for statistics: *UNHCR, 2009*

HOW MANY IMMIGRANTS ARE THERE?

What do we mean when we talk about immigrants? We know that they are people from other countries. If you live in a city, there may be neighborhoods where the people come from a different culture and country, such as Mexico or India. Although these people may be immigrants, we should be careful not to confuse **ethnic minorities** with immigrants.

■ In a well-established ethnic minority community, such as this one in Bradford, England, many of the people will be the children or grandchildren of immigrants, but not immigrants themselves.

What is an immigrant?

Immigrants are people who were born in another country. Ethnic minorities are people who have a different culture and way of life from the main culture in a country. Ethnic minorities are often second- or third-generation immigrants because their parents or grandparents were immigrants. Although the younger generation may continue to speak the language and follow the customs of the place where their parents were born, they were born in the country where they live now.

To find out how many immigrants there are, we need to know how many people are living in a country other than where they were born. Some will be settlers who have become citizens of the new country; others may be planning to return to their home country in the future. The United Nations says that anyone living outside their country of birth for more than one year is an immigrant. This is called the stock of immigrants in a country.

There are around 215 million people who live in a country other than the one where they were born. This sounds like a huge number, but it only represents about three percent of the world's population. Newspaper headlines and other media often suggest that immigration is growing and out of control. According to the United Nations, this is not the case. For the last 20 years at least, the proportion of the world's people who are immigrants has remained around three percent. However, as we shall see later in this chapter, some countries have far more immigration and emigration than others. The number of people moving into a country in any year is called the flow of immigrants.

LEGAL AND ILLEGAL IMMIGRANTS

We have already seen that not all immigrants move to their new countries legally. Legal immigrants need to have permission to live in their new home. This may involve getting an official **visa** that allows them to stay for a certain amount of time or to work in a particular job. Illegal immigrants are either people who cross the border without permission or those who remain in the country after their visa has expired (for more details on visas, see page 40). Illegal immigrants often do not appear on official records, so it is difficult to know exactly how many there are. It has been estimated that up to one in every five of the world's immigrants is illegal. The United States has the largest number of illegal immigrants at more than 11 million people.

Routes of migration

Immigrants' choices about where to move are influenced by many things. For economic migrants, the main concern is that they will be able to find work and will be better off than they would be in their home country.

Many migrants follow well-traveled routes when they choose to move. Mexican **emigrants** overwhelmingly choose to go to their powerful and wealthy neighbor to the north. The United States not only is Mexico's nearest neighbor but also has a large Mexican population that can support new immigrants. Many immigrants already have family in southern states like California and Texas and in larger cities across the country.

BUILDING DUBAI

Over the past few years, Dubai, a country located south of the Persian Gulf on the Arabian Peninsula, has seen a huge boom in construction funded by the country's oil wealth. The construction sites are staffed by migrant workers, particularly from India and Bangladesh. These people are recruited by companies in their home country. They can earn up to ten times what they would earn at home, but life in Dubai is hard. Workers live in very cramped conditions, with twelve workers sharing a room. The company often holds their passports. There have even been suggestions that, when the company they work for faces financial trouble, many workers are forced to work without pay. This is illegal, and campaigners say it is close to slavery.

■ Migrant workers in Dubai are often kept under tight control by the companies for which they work.

Family members are one of the main reasons why people move to a particular place. It is usually easier to get the visa necessary to move legally if the migrant already has family in that location. They can provide a place for the newly arrived immigrant to stay. The fact that immigrants often move to areas where there is already a large immigrant population means that immigration is not spread evenly across a country but concentrated in particular areas.

There are often historical reasons why migrants travel to certain countries. European countries like the United Kingdom and France once had numerous **colonies** around the world. Emigrants from former colonies may choose to move to these countries. France still attracts many immigrants from its former colonies in Africa. The United Kingdom is a popular destination for immigrants from India, Pakistan, Bangladesh, and Caribbean countries like Jamaica.

Which countries have the most immigrants?

The countries with the highest proportion of foreign-born people are Qatar and the United Arab Emirates in the Persian Gulf region. These countries had small populations before huge reserves of oil were discovered in the region. Fewer than 15 out of every 100 people in Qatar were born in the country. Most of the immigrants are temporary employees working in the oil or construction industries (see box on page 18). Many will return to their home countries after a few years.

Australia, New Zealand, and Canada also have a high proportion of foreign-born inhabitants. These developed countries are not densely populated and are keen to attract skilled immigrants.

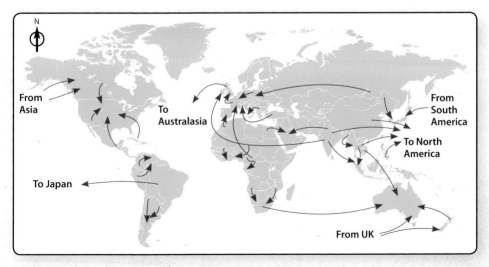

This map shows the main world migration routes.

The United States has far more foreign-born residents than any other country. The United Nations has estimated that in 2010, there were 42.8 million immigrants living there, more than three times as many as any other country. Immigrants to the United States come from many different countries, but those from Mexico make up 30 percent of the U.S. foreign-born population.

For much of the twentieth century, the United Kingdom and other western European countries had more emigrants leaving than immigrants arriving. That has changed in recent years. The U.K.'s foreign-born population reached 11 percent of the total in 2008, having tripled in size since 1980. Although immigrants from Ireland, India, and Pakistan had been moving to the United Kingdom for years, the early twenty-first century saw massive growth in immigration from eastern Europe, particularly Poland.

The European Union
One of the main reasons for this growth in immigration within Europe is the European Union (EU). The EU is an organization of 27 countries that cooperate economically and politically. Migration within Europe has increased dramatically, particularly from the former communist countries of eastern Europe to western countries like Germany and the United Kingdom.

Where are the world's refugees?
Refugees made up around 15 million of the world's immigrant population at the end of 2009. Although this is a small proportion of all immigrants, it is a huge number of people forced to leave their homes, often at a moment's notice, and live for years in camps on the borders of their homelands. Most refugees are in Pakistan and African countries. These countries are in turmoil themselves and face problems coping with huge, sudden waves of refugees.

Emigrant countries
Every immigrant who travels to another country is also an emigrant from somewhere. Countries with high emigration are not necessarily the poorest countries, although there are normally good economic reasons for people to move. They also have established emigration routes, such as the route from Mexico to the United States. The Philippines and India are also countries with high numbers of emigrants.

Polish shops on the streets of London are a sign of immigration to the U.K. from eastern Europe.

WESTERN COUNTRIES ARE "SWAMPED" BY IMMIGRANTS.

Newspaper headlines often use words like "swamped" to reflect people's worry that immigration is causing economic and cultural problems. What do you think, based on what you know about the numbers of immigrants?

Arguments for:
- The number of immigrants to countries like the United States and the United Kingdom has increased in recent years.
- Immigration is not divided evenly between countries—some countries receive many more immigrants than others.
- Within countries, some areas receive more immigrants than others, so those areas are more affected.
- Official figures hide the true impact of immigration because illegal immigrants and immigrants within regions like the EU are hard to track.

Arguments against:
- Total immigration has remained at around three percent of the world's population for many years.
- As populations in countries like Australia increase, immigrants make up a smaller proportion.
- Many immigrants are temporary workers and plan to return to their home countries.

THE EFFECTS OF IMMIGRATION

Immigration can certainly be a good thing for the immigrants who choose to live and work in a new country. However, immigration doesn't always work out. For many it can bring hardship, disappointment, or even death on the hazardous routes taken by illegal immigrants.

There is a lot of debate about the impact that immigration has on the destination countries. This debate falls into two parts: the economic impact and the effect of mass immigration on the culture of the host country.

Economic impact

One of the main arguments often used against immigrants is that they take jobs that would otherwise have gone to people born in the host country. If there are a fixed number of jobs, there will be more people applying for each one. In some cases, the job might be given to someone who is prepared to take less money or work longer hours. People who oppose immigration would say that immigrants are more likely to accept lower pay. One result is that the immigrant gets the job. Another possible outcome is that pay for that kind of job goes down because immigrants are prepared to do the job for less money.

▓ A high proportion of taxi drivers are immigrants. This is a dangerous job, with taxi drivers 30 times more likely to be killed on the job than other workers.

IMMIGRANTS TAKE JOBS FROM PEOPLE WHO WERE BORN IN THE COUNTRY.

Most experts agree that, in general, immigration can benefit the economy. There is less general agreement about the impact on jobs. Make up your own mind.

Arguments for:

- Many jobs that are done by recent immigrants could be done by people who are unemployed.
- Low-skilled immigrants are prepared to work for less money, which drives down wages for those who have jobs.
- High-skilled immigrants reduce opportunities for native graduates.

Arguments against:

- Low-skilled immigrants do essential jobs that other people don't want to do. Without immigrants, no one would do those jobs.
- Immigrants create jobs for other people. The more people there are, the more jobs are needed to provide them with services.
- Highly skilled migrants can help to raise overall standards of workers and train other people.

However, as we have seen, immigrants often find work in "difficult, dirty, and dangerous" jobs. Employers say that **native-born** workers often don't want to do those jobs, so low-skilled immigrants are filling essential jobs that would not be filled. Skilled migrants like doctors and engineers are doing work that benefits the whole of society, and they can help to develop those skills in the host country. Many developed countries that have restrictions on some immigration still want to attract skilled migrants.

Supporters of immigration also argue that immigrants create jobs. Immigrant workers use shops, transportation, and all the services that native-born people use, and they and their families pay to use these services, which in turn creates jobs for other people. It is true that many immigrants send money back to other family members in their home country, but they need to spend money to live in the host country.

When the economy is doing badly and people are losing their jobs, complaints about immigration are often louder. People argue that we need to find jobs for those who are already there before allowing more immigrants into the country. Governments are urged to crack down on illegal immigrants. But economic migrants will generally look to move to places where they know work is easy to find and avoid countries where unemployment is high. When a country is going through difficult economic times and there are fewer jobs, there will be fewer new immigrants, and many economic migrants will return home.

Paying taxes and claiming benefits

We all pay taxes to the government. People who earn money have to pay some of it to the government in the form of tax. We also pay taxes almost every time we spend money. In return for taxes, the government provides schools, health care, **welfare** benefits, and many other services.

Most legal immigrants pay taxes just like anyone else. A 2010 survey found that 75 percent of Americans believed that illegal immigrants were a drain on the economy because they do not pay taxes but use services like schools and hospitals. In fact many illegal immigrants pay taxes not only on what they buy, but also on what they earn. That is because the tax is taken away from their salary before they are paid. However, they are usually not able to claim **Social Security** benefits. The situation is much the same in other countries.

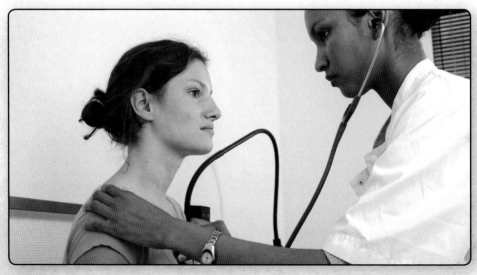

■ Immigrants put additional stress on services like health care, but they also help to pay for it with their taxes.

There are certainly some immigrants who avoid paying tax on what they earn, just as there are people in every country who break the law by not paying taxes. This is called the "black" or "shadow" economy. It may be that these people are committing crimes, such as dealing in illegal drugs, or doing legal jobs that are paid in cash so the government cannot track and tax their earnings.

Opponents of immigration claim that many immigrants move to wealthy countries with good welfare benefits so they can "sponge" off state benefits. Many studies have found that immigrants contribute at least as much to the economy as people born in that country.

Aging populations

Immigrants also make another very important contribution to the economies of developed countries. People in many European and other developed countries are having fewer children. If there is no immigration into these countries, their populations will start to shrink. You might think this sounds like a good idea.

Unfortunately, it's not all good news. Advances in health and medicine also mean that people are living longer than they ever have before. With the population shrinking and aging, there will be a lower proportion of people of working age in these countries. Working people earn the money and pay the taxes needed to pay for children to be educated and for older people to retire. Immigration is essential if these countries are to have enough people working and paying taxes to keep the economy going.

IMMIGRATION DURING A RECESSION

In late 2007, a **recession** began in the U.S. and other countries' economies around the world. During a recession, the economy shrinks, which normally means that people lose their jobs. Immigrants were affected by the recession as much as native-born workers. At the time of the recession, the flow of both legal and illegal immigrants declined. In the United Kingdom, many immigrants from elsewhere in the EU returned to their home countries.

Cultural impact

If we believe that our economy benefits from immigration, or even relies on it, what are the cultural effects of continuing immigration?

In 2007, a survey asked people in 47 countries around the world, both rich and poor, whether they were concerned about losing their way of life. In 46 of the countries, most people answered yes to that question (the exception was Sweden). In the same survey, more than 70 percent of people in the United States, United Kingdom, and most European countries said there should be more controls on immigration.

However, when they are asked about the impact of immigrants, only a **minority** of people say that this has been negative. Many people like the fact that immigration has brought many new things to their country. Think of all the foods from different countries that we can find in restaurants or supermarkets. Immigrants brought many of these foods with them. It is also worth remembering that some areas are home to more immigrants than others, so views may differ in different places.

DEBATE

SHOULD RIGHT-WING PARTIES BE INCLUDED IN MAINSTREAM POLITICS?

Many people argue that extreme right-wing groups hold views that are too extreme to be part of most political debates. What do you think?

Arguments for:

- Allowing these groups' views to be openly discussed will expose them as racists with beliefs that are unacceptable to most people.
- We all have freedom of speech, and we should defend this even if we oppose what people have to say.

Arguments against:

- Allowing people to express extreme views in the media may lead to violence against immigrants. Protecting people is more important than freedom of speech.
- If these groups are allowed to share a platform with **mainstream** politicians, it makes their views seem acceptable, when in fact these views only appeal to a minority of people.

People who like these developments point out that all cultures have been formed by different influences. American culture is a product of waves of immigration over many generations. Life in European countries has always been influenced by contact with each other and with other continents as Europeans traded and built empires overseas.

Culture shock

Many people are concerned that too much immigration is greatly changing their culture. These people often state that immigrants do not adapt to the culture of their new country, but continue to mix with people from their own country and speak their own language. People also argue that some immigrant groups hold views that are different from the views that are "normal" in the host country—for example, the role of women.

Extreme views

Extremist groups and political parties are active in many countries that have experienced mass immigration. Political parties like the British National Party and the Front National in France have tried to use people's worries about immigration to advance their racist views. These views include calling for a ban on immigration and returning immigrants to their home countries. Other extremist, far-right groups have used terrorism in their fight.

■ Mexican immigrants celebrate Cinco de Mayo in the United States. For many people, immigration enriches the culture of the host country.

Migration does not just affect countries that experience a lot of immigration. All immigrants are emigrants from somewhere else. Immigration affects some countries more than others, some countries are affected more by emigration.

Brain drain

One of the biggest concerns for countries that have high levels of emigration is that the people who leave are often young, ambitious and are more likely to be college graduates. These countries often have developing economies, so these are exactly the people they don't want to lose. Educating people costs money, and poorer countries cannot afford to educate people, only to have them find work overseas. Doctors are a good example. Amazingly, there are more Malawian doctors working in Manchester, England, than in Malawi itself. This "brain drain" particularly affects smaller countries where there are limited opportunities for graduates.

Emigration affects populations in other ways. Sometimes only one member of a family may emigrate to work overseas. This often means that many of the young men in a community have emigrated, placing extra pressures on wives and mothers to manage their households alone.

■ Money sent back home by someone living overseas can help lift people out of slums like this one in the Philippines.

Benefits of emigration

Emigration can also have positive effects. Developing countries often have fast-growing populations. Having too many people puts a lot of pressure on fragile economies. If people move to developed countries with shrinking populations, this makes sense for both sides.

Economic migrants move to places where they can earn more money. Often, much of this money is sent back to their home country to support family and friends. These payments, called **remittances**, can be a big part of the economies of smaller and poorer countries. Remittances from emigrants make up around 12 percent of the economy of the Philippines. Many wealthy emigrants may also fund community programs or start businesses in their home countries with the money they have made overseas.

TOP EMIGRANT COUNTRIES

The countries with the highest number of people born there but living in another country are Mexico, India, China, Bangladesh, and Turkey. China and India have populations of more than 1 billion people, so emigrants do not make up a big proportion of their total populations. Among Western countries, the United Kingdom has the most emigrants. Caribbean countries lose a high proportion of their people to emigration. Jamaica loses the most, with 39 percent of people emigrating.

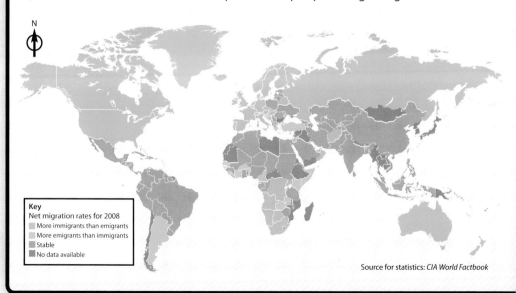

N

Key
Net migration rates for 2008
More immigrants than emigrants
More emigrants than immigrants
Stable
No data available

Source for statistics: *CIA World Factbook*

THE IMMIGRANT EXPERIENCE

The experiences of immigrants are quite varied. For many, immigration provides opportunities that would not have been available in their home countries. Others find that immigration doesn't live up to their expectations and return to their homelands after a short time.

Immigrants often follow established routes and are able to join family and friends in large communities from the same country. These are most often in big cities, although they may be in rural towns where people work in particular jobs, such as farming. Moving to an established community helps immigrants find work and a place to live. It also helps them to make friends with people who speak their language and share their culture.

Settling in

How easy it is for recent immigrants to feel comfortable in their new home will often depend on how the population in general views immigrants and how the immigrants respond to the culture of their new home. Some immigrants will be able to fit easily, or assimilate, into the new country, particularly if they come from a similar culture. Other groups will continue to follow their own culture or religion alongside the main culture of the country, creating a multicultural society.

Big cities usually accept immigrants much more easily than rural areas, which may not be used to seeing large numbers of immigrants. Other factors that may affect the reception given to immigrants include social and legal status, whether immigrant communities mix with the local community, and whether they speak the same language. People are usually more hostile to illegal or unskilled immigrants than they are to skilled migrants.

CASE STUDY

Moving to Kentucky

Most immigrants from Mexico settle in states close to the border, such as California, Texas, and Arizona, or in major cities like Chicago and New York. Immigrants who settle in more rural states have a very different experience. The four Ayala brothers from Michoacán, Mexico, moved at different times to earn money in the horse-racing industry of Kentucky. Living away from the larger Mexican communities, the brothers had to overcome cultural and language barriers that immigrants in big cities did not face. They sent money back to their family in Mexico, and some of the brothers hoped to return to their homeland, family, and friends. Juan, the second-oldest brother, married an American and has three children who don't speak Spanish.

■ Mexicans in rural states, like these dairy farm migrant workers in Colorado, face a different experience from that of immigrants who move to areas close to the Mexican border or to large cities.

"I'm better off here. About every month or two we can send something home, a bit of what's left over. But in Mexico, I have my family, all my friends....What I want more than anything is to be home soon."

Marcelo Ayala, a teenage Mexican immigrant in rural Kentucky

33

Immigrants often face many difficulties as they try to settle into their new home. Many immigrants say that not speaking the language has been their biggest problem when arriving in a new country. Speaking the language is important for finding work as well as in other aspects of life. Some immigrants, particularly refugees, may have left behind a very difficult situation and may be worried about friends or family.

Often immigrants will face racism and prejudice. In extreme cases, immigrants may be attacked or face insults or abuse. Racism may also lead to reduced opportunities for work or housing. This kind of prejudice is illegal in most countries but is still faced by many immigrants.

Muslim immigration since 9/11

Muslim immigrants and Muslim communities in Europe and North America have faced particular problems. On September 11, 2001, **terrorists** linked to Osama Bin Laden's network al-Qaeda crashed airplanes into buildings in New York City and Washington, D.C., killing more than 3,000 people. The attackers, who all died, had been granted visas to the United States, and three were still in the country even though their visas had expired.

The attacks led to many questions about immigration in general and immigrants from Muslim countries in particular. Although people recognized that the vast **majority** of Muslims in western countries opposed the attacks, and many innocent Muslims died, there was public debate about whether the values of Islam were compatible with Western society. Questions were asked about how security forces could police the threat from radical Islam without affecting ordinary Muslims. There were also some isolated attacks on innocent Muslims.

After 9/11 the United States and other Western governments introduced more limits on temporary visas and immigration. The number of people from Arab countries entering the United States for study or temporary work fell by around 70 percent in the years after 9/11. Many Muslims have strongly opposed the wars in Afghanistan and Iraq after 2001, and this has created tension between communities in many countries.

FRANCE AND THE VEIL

In 2010 France introduced a law that banned the wearing of the full veil, or *niqab*, by Muslim women in public places. This followed a ban in 2004 on girls wearing head scarves in French schools. Those who support the ban argue that it is a "medieval tradition" and is an example of foreigners not integrating into French society. Supporters of the small minority of French Muslims who wear the *niqab* argue that it is about freedom of choice. They also argue that many of those who wear the *niqab* were born in France. Who do you think is right about this?

■ The debate about the *niqab* in France raises questions about how far immigrants with strong religious and cultural traditions should go to adapt to the values of their new country.

CASE STUDY

Indian immigration to America

India is a country of more than 1 billion people. There are also large Indian populations, or people descended from Indian immigrants, in many countries including the United Kingdom, South Africa, Malaysia, and Saudi Arabia. Indians are one of the fastest-growing immigrant populations in the United States. The Indian-born population increased dramatically after 1990 and stood at more than 1.6 million people in 2010, making them the third-largest immigrant group in the United States, after those from Mexico and the Philippines.

The growth of the Indian population has happened at the same time as the growth in technology companies, particularly in the area known as Silicon Valley in California. A quarter of all male Indian immigrants work in information technology, and almost one in five Indian immigrants lives in California. Many Indian men and women are also employed in business and finance.

On average, Indian immigrants are better educated than other immigrants and even native-born Americans, with around 75 percent having a college degree. This makes Indian immigrants an important part of the workforce, although there are some who believe that technology companies would rather employ immigrants than well-qualified American workers.

Problems for Indian immigrants

Indian immigration to the United States has generally been successful, with fewer people living in poverty than other immigrant groups. However, the growing Indian population has had some problems. In the wake of the terrorist attacks of 9/11, there were a few cases of Indians being attacked—they were mistaken for Arabs. Many of those attacked were not even Muslim.

The dramatic growth in immigration from India since 1990 has brought its own problems. Lawmakers have raised the costs of new visas for companies that employ a majority of foreign workers. Indian companies that provide services in the United States claim that they are being deliberately targeted.

Around the world

Many Indians traveled to the United Kingdom after India became independent in 1947, and Indians remain the largest foreign-born group there. The Persian Gulf has also been a traditional destination for Indian workers. India receives more remittances from Indians living overseas than any other country.

High-tech immigrant Sanjay Mavinkurve always wanted to live in the United States. Sanjay was born in India and lived in Saudi Arabia as a child. Sanjay attended Harvard University, where he worked on an early version of Facebook. In 2003 he joined Google, becoming one of hundreds of immigrants working for the software company. Google has made Sanjay rich and successful.

But not everything has worked out well. Sanjay lives in Toronto, Canada, and travels to Google's office in California because of problems getting a visa for his wife to live and work in the United States. Campaigners and politicians are calling for fewer foreign-born workers at technology companies. Sanjay has worked hard and paid his taxes, but feels unloved by the country he dreamed about as a child.

■ Indian immigrants have made a big contribution to the development of U.S. technology companies. Many Indians are also bringing the skills they have learned back to their homeland to benefit India's growing economy.

THE IMMIGRATION INDUSTRY

With more than 200 million people living outside the country of their birth, migration is a big business. An industry has grown up around people's desire to move to a new country. Much of this industry is within the law. Travel agents, interpreters, and lawyers earn a living by organizing legal immigration. There are also people within immigrant communities who spend at least some of their time organizing and providing jobs and places to stay for new immigrants. The desperation of some people to reach Europe or North America leads them to put their trust in people who operate outside the law, such as people smugglers and those who supply false documents.

DANGERS OF PEOPLE SMUGGLING

A horrific example of the dangers of people smuggling was discovered at the British port of Dover in 2000. Customs officials suspected that a truck that was supposed to be carrying tomatoes was actually being used to smuggle illegal goods. When officials opened the back door of the truck, they found the bodies of 58 Chinese immigrants. Two men survived the terrible ordeal and spoke of people banging on the sides of the truck and clawing at the locked doors as the air inside started to run out. An air vent had been accidentally closed, meaning that not enough air could get into the truck. One survivor said he had paid a Chinese gang about $30,000 for the journey from Beijing, China, to the United Kingdom.

Migrant workers are often recruited in their own countries before traveling to their destinations. This is particularly the case for work on construction projects that may use a large number of migrant workers. The company, or **broker**, organizes transportation and paperwork, and has a lot of control over the workforce. Workers often pay large sums to brokers to get these jobs, which may be deducted from what they earn. They also put themselves in the hands of the brokers with very little direct knowledge about the job itself. Conditions in their new home can be much worse than they expect.

People smuggling

More dangerous are smugglers who bring people across borders illegally. Immigrants who wish to cross borders illegally will pay a fee to the smugglers to transport them across the border, often in very dangerous ways. Smuggled immigrants may enter a country in the back of a truck or by bribing border officials. Smuggling gangs are often involved in other kinds of illegal activities such as smuggling drugs. Migrants who put themselves in the hands of people smugglers probably know the risks they are taking. However, the smugglers may offer one of the few ways out of extreme poverty.

■ Many immigrants feel that the dangers of being smuggled across the border in the back of a truck are worth it for the potential rewards of getting to their chosen country.

Smuggling routes

More illegal immigrants cross the border between Mexico and the United States than any other border. Smugglers on the U.S.-Mexico border are called coyotes. They offer to guide immigrants through the desert or across the treacherous Rio Grande River. Most of these illegal immigrants are Mexicans, but immigrants from across Central and South America also try to cross this border.

The main route for entry into the European Union is via Turkey. It is very difficult to know the size of the people smuggling industry, but one estimate claims that people smuggling across the Turkish border is worth $300 million every year. Other illegal immigrants are smuggled into the EU across the Mediterranean Sea, either from Morocco to Spain or from Croatia and Albania to Italy. Around 2,000 immigrants die crossing the Mediterranean Sea every year. Land borders are usually more difficult to police than sea crossings, and many illegal immigrants enter through Europe's long eastern land border.

■ Australia has no land borders with other countries. In 2001, hundreds of Afghan asylum seekers were picked up from a sinking boat by the *MV Tampa*. The ship was refused permission to land in Australia.

Why is smuggling so common?

Why do so many people put themselves in the hands of smugglers or fall for the deceptions of people traffickers? Smuggling operations are well established, and people know that the route is difficult, dangerous, and expensive. There is always the risk of being stopped at the border and sent back to where they came from. Around 800,000 illegal immigrants are caught at the U.S.-Mexican border every year, although this figure started to fall in 2007. Below are some reasons why immigrants work with smugglers.

- Most of the world's population lives in extreme poverty, and the determination to seek a better life for themselves and their families leads them to take risks that those who do not face such hardship do not have to take.

- Many people believe that tighter immigration controls lead people to choose smugglers rather than legal means. Some would argue that immigration controls do not really reduce immigration but force people to take dangerous illegal routes. The next chapter looks in more detail at ways of controlling immigration.

- Immigrants often follow routes that others in their community have followed, and smugglers hold a powerful position in many of those communities. This may mean that in some cases, people are not aware of the legal routes of migration, although these routes are often only open to skilled migrants.

PEOPLE TRAFFICKING

People trafficking is different from smuggling, as the people involved are not willing participants. People trafficking sometimes involves kidnapping, but usually desperate people are tricked by offers of work overseas. Most victims are women and children, who are forced into crime or are exploited sexually. People trafficking is particularly common in southeast Asia. The U.S. State Department has estimated that people trafficking affects 800,000 people every year.

CONTROLLING IMMIGRATION

In most countries, governments are elected by their citizens. Immigration is often one of the major issues discussed at elections. In recent years, **opinion polls** have shown that the majority of voters at elections have opposed further immigration. Business leaders are usually in favor of immigration, saying that immigrants are important to fill jobs. Governments need to strike a balance between responding to concerns about too much immigration and allowing enough immigration to provide the skills the country needs and that benefit the economy.

Passports and visas

Passports and visas are the basic documents that indicate who can live or work in a country. If you travel to another country, you will need to have a passport to prove who you are and that you are a citizen of your home country. Depending on where you're traveling and the reason for your visit, you may also need a visa. Visas are official documents that enable people to enter another country. You may not need a visa to go on vacation, but you will probably need one if you wish to work or study in another country. Passports, visas, and border controls are used to maintain legal migration and track the movement of people.

People who want to live in another country legally will need a visa. Most countries that get a lot of immigrants have restrictions on who can be given a visa. Some of the main categories include:

- Skilled migrants: These are people who have skills that are needed in the country's economy. Applications are based on things like qualifications, age, previous earnings, and language skills.
- Students
- Families: Many countries try to keep families together.

- Random requests: The United States issues visas to 50,000 random applicants each year in a lottery.
- Temporary workers

There may be limits on the numbers of each type of visa that can be issued, to keep legal immigration at a certain level.

Illegal immigrants

Countries put huge efforts into controlling migration, but there are still millions of illegal immigrants. How have countries tried to control illegal immigration?

- Deportation: When illegal immigrants are caught, they are often deported, or sent back to the countries they came from. The United States imprisons some illegal immigrants in order to deter repeat offenders.
- Employment laws: Employers must check if people they hire are legally allowed to work. Employers are often fined if they have hired illegal workers.
- Legalizing immigrants: Countries will sometimes declare an **amnesty** for groups of illegal immigrants, such as those who have been in the country for many years. This is very controversial as it is seen to reward illegal immigrants, but governments argue that they can protect immigrants from exploitation and also collect taxes from them. Many industries rely on illegal workers, so legalization is a good solution for them.

■ On June 22, 1948, the ex-troopship *Empire Windrush* arrived from Jamaica with 482 Jamaicans on board emigrating to Britain.

Refugees and asylum seekers

Most countries agree to follow the United Nations Convention on the Status of Refugees. This means that they must protect refugees and not send them to countries where they may be persecuted. Many refugees are found in developing countries (see pages 12 to 13) close to their home countries, but some refugees will be sent to other countries.

Asylum seekers are people who do not yet have refugee status. They are often unable to return to their home countries because those countries will not accept them or they have no passports. Asylum seekers are unable to work in their new country until their claim for asylum, or protection in another country, has been heard. They are often seen as economic migrants rather than refugees, and only around 10 percent of asylum applications are successful.

Policing the borders

Countries that wish to control immigration have to spend a lot of money policing their borders. This is particularly difficult for countries that have long land borders, such as the United States and Mexico (see pages 44 to 45). Countries surrounded by water, such as the United Kingdom, Australia, and New Zealand, present an extra obstacle to illegal immigrants.

For many countries, controlling immigration is also about providing security for people. Tighter border controls are seen as an important part of the fight against terrorism.

■ Refugees and asylum seekers usually have very little time to pack and can only bring just a few of their belongings. If you had to quickly leave your country, what would you choose to take?

SHOULD WE HAVE OPEN BORDERS?

Most people believe that some immigration controls are essential for many reasons, including to control the movement of criminals. Many argue for even tougher controls than are already in place. Others argue that people should be allowed to move freely between countries and that this will bring greater prosperity for all.

Arguments for:

- Everyone should have a right to escape poverty or persecution. For many people, migration is the best way of finding a better life.
- Immigration brings many economic benefits, including filling essential jobs that would otherwise not be filled and paying taxes that enable governments to provide essential services.
- Currently, people who are not able to migrate legally take difficult and dangerous illegal routes. These people will move anyway, so it would be better if this was within the law.
- Policing national borders costs huge amounts of money that could be spent on useful things like education and health care.

Arguments against:

- Allowing free immigration would lead to wealthy countries being swamped by huge numbers of immigrants, destroying the culture of the people who already live there.
- More people would lose their jobs or get paid less because of competition from immigrants.
- Poorer nations would lose even more of their best and brightest people than they do at present, as they would all go where they could earn more money.
- Open borders would be bad for our security and would help criminals and terrorists.

Freedom of movement already happens in the European Union. Do you think this has been a success? It has certainly led to more immigration to wealthier countries, but has this been a good or bad thing? Think about the issues and decide for yourself.

CASE STUDY

Border Patrol

In August 2010, U.S. president Barack Obama signed a bill to increase security on the Mexican border. The bill would add 1,000 border patrol agents to the force of more than 17,000 that patrol the border. It would also increase electronic surveillance using cameras, motion sensors, and unmanned **drone** aircraft to watch the border.

More legal and illegal immigrants cross this border than any other. It is also a major crossing point for trade, not just in legal goods but also drugs and weapons. The U.S. Border Patrol is responsible for policing the border, not just to prevent illegal immigration but also to guard against terrorists, terrorist weapons, and the trade in drugs.

Calls to strengthen the Mexican border have increased since 9/11, and the number of border patrol agents almost doubled from 2000 to 2010. The border patrol has always been in the frontline of the fight against illegal immigration. High metal fences protect many popular crossing areas around major cities, such as the crossing point between Juarez in Mexico and El Paso in Texas. However, the blocking of these crossing points has led to more immigrants crossing the border in isolated desert areas.

Does border control work?

The United States spends billions of dollars every year policing the Mexican border. Does this huge effort have an effect? Illegal immigration across the border fell substantially between 2007 and 2009. Part of this fall was due to increased security and the resulting increased cost of smuggling. However, this was a period when work was harder to find in the United States, so economic migrants might have been less likely to take the risky journey. The violent drug war on the Mexican side of the border also made crossing more dangerous.

Many people point out that strengthening the border is only part of the solution. If people have enough reason to migrate, they will take the risk and some will get through, as they have in the past. People argue that resources also need to be directed at tackling the causes of immigration, such as poverty and the wider immigration system.

■ The high metal fences that mark much of the Mexican border are supported by high-tech surveillance materials and a growing army of border guards.

Drug wars

In August 2010, the same month the United States passed a bill to strengthen the Mexican border, the dead bodies of 72 illegal immigrants from across Central and South America were found in northeastern Mexico. The immigrants had been murdered by Mexican drug gangs. The warring gangs steal money that the immigrants are carrying to pay people smugglers who will help them cross the border into the United States. Some of these immigrants are forced to work for the gangs. Because they are illegal immigrants in Mexico, the victims are unknown to the authorities and get little protection. This is just one result of the murderous war for control of the drug trade that has made the Mexican side of the border one of the world's most dangerous places.

IMMIGRATION AND THE MEDIA

As we have seen throughout this book, many of the issues around immigration are complex. However, if you look at media reports about immigration, the issues may seem much less complex. Although some of the printed, online, and broadcasting media give balanced coverage of the issues around immigration, there are TV channels, newspapers, and, particularly, websites and **blogs** that give a much less balanced view.

Broadcast media and newspapers

Media outlets would argue that they reflect the views of their audience. Opinion polls often show that, in countries including the United States and the United Kingdom, the majority of people are concerned about the level of immigration. Newspapers and TV channels are funded by advertising. To attract these advertisers, they must appeal to a particular audience and reflect their views. Most people would not read a newspaper for very long if it continually expressed views with which they strongly disagreed.

Websites and blogs

Online media are slightly different, although all major news organizations and newspapers have an online presence. Whereas traditional media like newspapers and TV programs are very expensive to produce and have to appeal to a wide audience, online blogs and websites cost almost nothing to produce. Views expressed on a website may just be the view of one person who had the time and know-how to post them. Many blogs and websites are useful, informative, and entertaining, but some can be biased and inaccurate.

Media responsibility

Australia has more than 4.5 million immigrants. Immigration has helped the country's population to double over the past 50 years. This has led to some tensions. In December 2005, riots erupted on a Sydney beach following a disagreement between Lebanese-Australians and lifesavers, in which the two sides had exchanged taunts and insults. Following the riots, there were accusations that newspapers and talk radio presenters had used anti-Muslim and anti-Lebanese language designed to raise tensions in the situation, including printing the messages and slogans written and said by the white Australian rioters. Does the media have a responsibility not to provoke violence between different cultures?

TWO SIDES TO EVERY STORY

As the following headlines show, different media may have very different views on immigration, depending on the audience to which they are trying to appeal.

"Illegal Immigration to U.S. Slows Sharply" (Wall Street Journal, September 1, 2010)

"Study Shows Illegal Immigrants from Mexico Staying Put Despite Overall Decline" (foxnews.com, September 2, 2010)

■ Asylum seekers are often a very hot topic in the media. These asylum seekers were detained in Malta while trying to reach Europe from north Africa.

Attracting immigrants

As well as reporting and commenting on the debates about immigration, the media also has a direct influence on immigration. Many people decide to emigrate to the United States or Europe because of things they have seen in films or on TV. A bit like a vacation brochure, these will often present a very positive picture of the country where they are set. Potential immigrants may also see advertising for consumer goods. Advertising is designed to sell things and will always show things in the best possible light.

Countries that attract a lot of immigration know the power of the media. The United States and Australia have both produced advertisements to warn immigrants about the dangers of traveling illegally to their countries.

SPOTTING MEDIA BIAS

When researching information about immigration and other controversial topics, you need to be alert to media bias. Think about the source of the news and how the story is being presented.

- Look at the source of the story: Is it designed to appeal to a particular audience? Is the author trying to persuade you or give a balanced report? The story may be biased just because of who the author is. A reporter in one country may think he is balanced but may have a very different view from one in another country.

- Notice the facts selected: An author may only use facts that agree with his point of view. Other sources may include very different facts.

- Notice the language used: Words used in headlines and stories might be chosen to give a particular impression. For instance, saying that someone has been "seized" is very different from saying someone has been "rescued," but both words could be describing the same event from different points of view.

- Don't be blinded by statistics: They can often be used to back up many different points of view. Language can also be used to give a particular interpretation of the numbers. A rise in numbers of immigrants could be presented as a "slight increase" or a "massive rise," depending on the author's point of view.

Media for immigrants

The media also provides ways for immigrants to connect with each other. Many larger immigrant groups have their own radio or TV stations. Immigrant communities can use the Internet to connect with people in their home countries in ways that would not have been possible even 20 years ago. New media enables even small immigrant communities to create their own websites and newsletters.

Whatever we may think of the coverage of immigration in the media, immigration will always be a feature of our society, just as it has been in the past. Over the coming years, media and technology will continue to bring the world closer together. Countries will continue to try and balance the cultural concerns about immigration with their economic needs. There are no easy answers about immigration and how much immigration is the right amount. That is why immigration is such a hot topic in the media and when people vote at elections. Hopefully this book will help you to make up your own mind about some of those issues.

■ Sometimes immigrants choose to live in neighborhoods with other people from their home country (like New York City's Chinatown).

IMMIGRATION FACTS

These pages show the immigrant populations of different countries around the world. There is also a list of cities that have more than one million immigrants.

	Population	Immigrants/foreign-born population	Where do immigrants come from?
Australia	21,512,000	4,711,490 (21.9%)	UK, New Zealand, Italy, Vietnam, China. Immigrants from Asia are fastest-growing groups.
Canada	33,890,000	7,202,340 (21.3%)	UK, China (including Hong Kong), India. Immigrants from Asia are fastest-growing groups.
France	62,637,000	6,684,842 (10.7%)	Portugal, Algeria, Morocco
Germany	82,057,000	10,758,061 (13.1%)	Turkey, Italy, Greece, Poland
India	1,214,464,000	5,436,012 (0.4%)	Bangladesh, Pakistan, Nepal
Saudi Arabia	26,246,000	7,288,900 (27.8%)	Other Arab and Middle Eastern countries, India, Pakistan, Bangladesh

South Africa	50,492,000	1,862,889 (3.7%)	Neighboring countries in southern Africa, including Zimbabwe. The South African government claims that official figures do not include 3 million immigrants from Zimbabwe.
Spain	45,317,000	6,377,524 (14.1%)	Romania (increased more than 1,000% from 2000 to 2008), Morocco, Ecuador, UK
United Kingdom	61,899,000	6,451,711 (10.4%)	India, Poland, Pakistan, Ireland, Germany (many of these are British citizens who were born to military parents stationed in Germany)
United States	317,641,000	42,813,281 (13.5%)	Mexico, Philippines, India, China

Cities with more than 1 million immigrants

Chicago, USA

Dallas, USA

Dubai, United Arab Emirates

Houston, USA

Hong Kong, China

Jeddah, Saudi Arabia

London, U.K.

Los Angeles, USA

Melbourne, Australia

Miami, USA

Moscow, Russia

New York, USA

Paris, France

Riyadh, Saudi Arabia

San Francisco, USA

Singapore

Sydney, Australia

Toronto, Canada

Washington D.C., USA

Source: Migration Policy Institute

GLOSSARY

amnesty the granting of a pardon to a number of individuals

ancestor person who lived before us from whom we are descended

asylum seeker someone who asks for asylum (protection) but has not yet been accepted by another country as a refugee

blog (weblog) website or section of a website that can be regularly updated like a journal

broker someone who organizes buying and selling for others. A broker might hire workers to work on a project in another country.

colony country or place ruled by another one

culture customs and beliefs that are shared by a group of people, including language, food, and music

developed country country where industry and the economy are fully developed. These are usually wealthier countries, such as the United States, the United Kingdom, major European countries, Canada, Japan, and Australia.

developing country poorer country where the economy is not yet fully developed. Examples include many countries in Africa, Asia, and South America.

drone unmanned plane controlled from the ground that can be used for surveillance over hostile territory or to attack enemies

emigrant person who leaves his or her country to live in another

ethnic minority group that shares a common culture or national background that is different from most of the people in a country

faction small group of people within a larger one. Different factions will often disagree with each other.

immigrant someone who lives in a country that is different from the one he or she was born in

indigenous first people to live in a certain place. Aboriginal Australians were the first people to live in Australia.

mainstream opinions held or actions done by a majority of people

majority biggest part of something

migrant anyone who moves from one country to another

migrate to move from one country to another

minority smaller part of something

native-born someone born in the country where they live

opinion poll organized survey to find out what people think on a certain issue

persecution being picked on or attacked by someone repeatedly. Refugees often have to leave because they are persecuted by other groups in their home country.

poverty lack of money or possessions

recession period where an economy performs badly. It is usually more difficult to find work in a recession because people lose their jobs.

refugee person who is forced to move from home because of war or out of fear of being harmed

remittance money that emigrants send back to family and friends in their home country. Remittances make up a significant part of the economy of countries like the Philippines and Mexico.

Social Security a U.S. government program that includes old-age and survivors insurance, state unemployment insurance, and old-age assistance

skilled migrant immigrant who has a high level of education or particular skills and training that are required by the new country, such as doctors or engineers

Taliban political movement in Afghanistan that practices a very strict form of Islam. The Taliban previously formed the government of Afghanistan and has been fighting with the United States, United Kingdom, and their allies since 2001.

terrorist anyone who seeks to achieve political goals by carrying out acts of violence on civilians

United Nations organization that includes most countries in the world and was formed after World War II to manage disputes between countries and prevent wars

visa document that allows someone to legally enter another country. There are different types of visas depending on the reason the person is moving.

welfare payments that are made by the government to people who are unable to earn money because of unemployment, sickness, or other reasons

FURTHER INFORMATION

Books

Ambrosek, Renee. *America Debates United States Policy on Immigration*. New York: Rosen Publishing, 2008.

Donovan, Sandy. *The Hispanic American Experience*. USA TODAY Cultural Mosaic. Minneapolis: 21st Century Books, 2010.

Hernandez, Roger E. *Immigration*. Gallup Major Trends and Events. Broomall, PA: Mason Crest, 2007.

Levy, Janey. *Illegal Immigration and Amnesty*. In the News. New York: Rosen Publishing, 2010.

Morrow, Robert. *Immigration*. USA TODAY Debate: Voices and Perspectives. Minneapolis: 21st Century Books, 2010.

Shuster, Kate. *Should Immigration Be Restricted?* What Do You Think? Chicago: Heinemann Library, 2008.

Websites

Most major news organizations will include regular coverage of immigration issues. Some of the most reliable are:

http://topics.nytimes.com/top/reference/timestopics/subjects/i/immigration-and-emigration/index.html
The *New York Times* section on immigration.

http://topics.cnn.com/topics/immigration
CNN's website has a section containing news and videos on immigration.

www.migrationinformation.org
The Migration Policy Institute's site contains all sorts of free information about immigration, including country profiles and other data.

http://www.cbp.gov/xp/cgov/border_security/
The U.S. Customs and Border Protection Agency is part of the Department Homeland Security. Its website includes information and the latest news about the U.S. border and immigration.

www.unhcr.org.
The UNHCR is the official United Nations body that protects refugees around the world. Find out more about its work.

http://pstalker.com/migration/index.php
Stalker's Guide to International Immigration gives a positive view of the benefits of immigration and includes useful data.

When looking at web resources, be on the lookout for bias or sites that are promoting a particular point of view.

Topics for further research

- Immigration in your area: Do you live in an area with lots of immigrants? Why did people move to your area? How has this benefitted the area? Are there also problems caused by immigration? How do local people feel?

- Refugees around the world: Why do people become refugees? Every year there are crises that mean people have to leave their homes. Investigating these causes may lead you to find out about conflicts and problems that don't make the news.

INDEX